What's Next?

Emily Hyman

BookLeaf Publishing
India | USA | UK

What's Next? © 2023 Emily Hyman

All rights reserved.

No part of this publication may be reproduced, stored in a retrieval system, or transmitted, in any form or by any means, electronic, mechanical, photocopying, recording or otherwise, without the prior written permission of the presenters.

Emily Hyman asserts the moral right to be identified as author of this work.

Presentation by *BookLeaf Publishing*

Web: www.bookleafpub.com

E-mail: info@bookleafpub.com

ISBN: 9789358310146

First edition 2023

DEDICATION

I dedicate this book to my little growing family. We may not always have it all but we can do it all together if we stay comitted to one another.

The Unexpected

We didn't mean for this to happen.
Please catch me.
Drowning in a sea
of unforsaken emotion.

One...
Two....
Three?
Too many.

A night is all it took.
The gates broke,
away went the cloak.
Everything poured.

Hours turned to days,
not that short.
Time blended.
A voice inside screams.

No one there to help.
No one there to listen.
No vision
of hope.

That's how it began.

The start to the journey
of what is
the unexpected.

Trapped Inside

Put on these clothes.
Identity stripped.
Taking the blows
with those socks that are gripped.

Panick begins.
Not sure how to reach out.
Closing walls of sins.
Please let me blackout.

"You have to eat now."
"Come eat or you can't."
If only my stomach would allow,
rather throw up in the plant.

Quick introduction
leads to stares.
There is no production
just tears and empty chairs.

"Take these meds,
you won't make it without them."
Negativity spreads.
Nerves numb.

"We may need to keep you longer."
Panick arises again.
All these promises to leave had me stronger,
it all went down the drain.

Why give false hope?
Home is calling me.
Struggling to hand onto the rope,
I need my baby.

Someone break the chains.
Provide these people with trust.
Anxiety runs through my veins
as the meeting is discussed.

Take me home.
Keep me safe and sound.
Keep me in our dome
where we both can be found.

Chaotic Happiness

Should have taken it slow
but only we know.
The rest of the world can judge
as my body begins to pudge.

No,
not planned.
So?
The news is still grand.

Dad knew before mother.
Then, we discovered you were a brother.
Sissy will grow to love you.
She already loves the blue.

Time is ticking down.
Mom is really sore.
Counting until the day for the gown,
ready for the maternity floor.

Almost time...
ready to climb.
A new beginning,
memories imprinting.

Cornered

Leave?
Stay?
Breathe,
pray.

We've
fought about pay.
Crying in my sleeve,
I just need to grieve.

Please help decide.
I don't know if I can do this.
It is not about pride
but about the bliss.

Unsure who to confide.
I just don't want to miss
the opening stride.
Someone be my guide.

I love being a mom,
don't get me wrong.
Trying to stay calm
amongst the two sided prong.

Maybe there is a psalm
or a song?
We could make it into a rom-com
or let it blow up like a bomb.

Locked Opinions

Why have children now?
Why do something so selfish?
I respond with a furrowed brow,
"Mind your business."
Don't be elfish.
Where is the fairness?

My life does not concern you.
My children are safe and happy,
with big smiles,
that I know to be true.
Go pay attention
to your own life that may be trashy.

Negative Positivity

Cheers to another day.
Cheers to something else you have to say.
Cheers to fighting about pay.
Cheers to a never ending fray.

Cheers to this parenting.
Cheers to always fighting.
Cheers to never giving.
Cheers to always taking.

Cheers to your needs met.
Cheers to the constant fret.
Cheers to the nag of a pet.
Cheers to the win you always get.

Freedom Bound

Taste that?
It is sweet freedom.
A break well needed.
Hear that?
It is silence.
A breath of fresh air.
Do you feel that?
It is the relief of stress.
A moment of continuous hope.
Do you smell that?
It is victory.
A sliver of freedom.
Do you see that?
It is the end.
A release of the chains.

Mental Scars

The thoughts never die.
The experience pry.

Each event so clear.
Always something to fear.

Just getting by.
All we can do is try.

No going backwards now.
Forwards is set to plow.

Forever on the brain.
It is an endless game.

Justify the Means

It is only a break,
you can do it.
For goodness sake,
does not mean you have to quit.

It is just a few years.
You can go back.
Cheers.
You'll get back on track.

A bump in the road,
that much I know.
In the mode,
to applaud the show.

Diploma in hand.
Success just the beginning.
It is all part that is planned.
Emotions spinning.

Almost to the end.
Just enjoy this time now.
Before it is their turn to send.
Off in the educational wow.

Little Gifts

First we were expecting
until we had the misfortune of loss.
Then we were re-directing
and got a mini girl boss.

One year later
and here we are again
expecting greater,
a little man to gain.

Looking down the road,
the future is exciting.
It is like gold,
stars in writing.

Exposed

Skin to skin.
Heart beats match.
You, my kin,
can always attach.

Privacy gone.
This is my life.
Up night to dawn,
just the housewife.

People come in and out.
Always passing through.
One little shout,
no one has a clue.

Alone.
Yet oversimulated.
Grabbing the phone
trying not to get frustrated.

A call is all it takes
for someone to listen.
Nothing wrong with breaks.
Time of glisten.

Glimpse of Color

Black and white,
what a sight.
See it come.
Where is it from?

Motion pictures
playing literatures.
Dreams on screen
feels serene.

Dancing in the distance
of existence.
A red umbrella
with a gal and a fella.

Love is in the air
so good not to stare.
Something to crave
confidence and brave.

Black and white,
what a sight.
Never would imagine,
only pathum.

Glimpse of color.
Just like mother,
with lips so red,
it marks the kiss before bed.

Hidden Love

Meet me by the bay
we can chat and lay
on the sandy beach we stay
but words never say.

Feelings of devotion.
Heart of emotion.
World spins in slow motion,
hearing waves of the ocean.

Don't let go
we can lay low.
Wrapped in a box and bow,
no one has to know.

Our time,
away it climbs.
Feels like a crime.
We are in our prime.

No one knows,
our love that grows.
It shows
tides of highs and lows.

Keep me locked away,
in a treasure chest in the clay.
People will prey.
Nothing will ruin this day.

What's Next?

Can we start over?
Trying to find us.
Do you want a different lover?
About to bust.

Tensions hit.
Then a calm slides in.
Hold on and sit.
Down goes the chin.

Where did we go?
How did this happen?
Our love was like a show.
Heart broken and sadden.

Will we get back?
What do we have to do?
Before we throw the sack
and find something new.

Efforts are failing.
Time is creeping.
Does not mean I am bailing,
just here sitting and weeping.

Unsure what to do
or what to say in person or text.
Just be honest and true.
What's next?

Ghosted

Passing through walls
whistles of ambience falls.
Nothing to see
except a swaying tree.

Dead limbs drop.
Step back a hop.
Unsure feeling.
Graves are stealing.

Bodies once here
now just near.
More dirt
hidden by a grass skirt.

Underestimated.
The shaded.
Grounds of earth
once were birth.

Up in the sky.
The souls fly.
Soaring free.
Above the ghost tree.

Remember When?

Remember when we met?
I still remember all the sweat.
Remember being childish?
Pushing and shoving, so wildish.

Remember our first date?
We brought another mate.
Remember the nerves?
All our feelings in reserves.

Remember our first kiss?
A memory to never miss.
Remember when we fully fell?
We wer under such a spell.

Remember when we went camping?
Beginning the books of stamping .
Remember when we used to cuddle?
Melted the heart to a puddle.

Remember how we used to be?
So care free.
Remember?
We said forever and always.

Remember our saying?
It keeps us praying.
Remember no matter the weather?
In it together.

Forward Only

Don't reverse.
Keep driving.
Forward only.

Don't look for worse.
Keep striving.
Forward only.

No looking back.
The past is the past.
Forward only.

Stay on the track.
No being last.
Forward only.

Delivered Hope

Crystals align
feeling better than fine.
A message so clear,
nothing to fear.

Everything will work out
no need to shout.
The world does not play fair
but wait on the care.

Life is wonderful,
beautiful.
Keep up the hope,
never going down slope.

Breakdown

Strength.
Weakness.
Bravery.
Fear.

Length.
Uniqueness.
Savory.
Tear.

Countless words,
sounds absurd.
Actions
bring satisfactions.

Captured

Picture perfect.
Memories to dissect.
Here I am,
an outspoken lamb.

Who am I?
Doors to pry.
More than mom, I think?
Just need to link.

Take the time,
find the rhyme.
Finding who I am
to come out on top like BAM!

Focused

Testifying my devotion.
Do better, be better.
No more commotion,
written in a letter.

The statement set.
A new direction.
A high bet,
more selection.

Here I stand to say
for my family I will be
the one to stay.
Everyone will see.

Inspiration
is the drug.
Taking station
without pulling out the rug.

In addition,
the hope is to them proud.
It is the mission,
speaking out loud.

Goals will be made.
Mama will instill
a helping aide.
Envious skill.

Printed in the USA
CPSIA information can be obtained
at www.ICGtesting.com
LVHW010852230224
772522LV00013B/747